THE PORTABLE 7 HABITS™

Sharing Ideas, Insights, and Understanding

Other Portable 7 Habits Books

Choice: Choosing the Proactive Life You Want to Live
Vision: Defining Your Destiny in Life
Purpose: Focusing on What Matters Most
Abundance: Fulfilling Your Potential for Success
Synergy: Connecting to the Power of Cooperation
Renewal: Nourishing Body, Mind, Heart, and Soul

Other Books from Franklin Covey

The 7 Habits of Highly Effective People
The 7 Habits of Highly Effective Families
The 7 Habits of Highly Effective Teens
The 7 Habits of Highly Effective Teens Journal
Daily Reflections for Highly Effective Teens
Daily Reflections for Highly Effective People
Living the 7 Habits
Loving Reminders for Kids
Loving Reminders for Couples
Loving Reminders for Families
Loving Reminders Teen to Teen
Loving Reminders to Make Kids Laugh
Quotes and Quips

Franklin Covey
2200 West Parkway Boulevard
Salt Lake City, Utah 84119-2099

Concept: Cheryl Kerzner
Design: Jenny Peterson
Illustration: Tammy Smith
Written and compiled by Debra Harris
Contributors: John Crowley, Ann Hobson, Sunny Larson, Shelley Orgill

Manufactured in United States of America

ISBN 1-929494-13-0

CONTENTS

When we are upset, we hear with *fear muffs* on our ears. We hear with our broken hearts, our shattered egos, and our anger. At times like this, harmless little words take on great big meanings, and the smallest, most innocent gestures become life-threatening movements. You may feel like you are being attacked when you are actually being consoled. You may think you are being criticized when you are really being supported. If you know you are upset or feeling vulnerable, ask people what they are saying before you jump to a conclusion about what they have said.

—IYANLA VANZANT

INTRODUCTION

How others communicate with you and how well you listen and respond correlates directly with the quality of your relationships. All it takes to become a good listener is giving others your sustained attention and having the desire to hear the meaning behind the words before jumping in with your own autobiography.

In *Trust: Sharing Ideas, Insights, and Understanding*, we've simplified the powerful principles behind *The 7 Habits of Highly Effective People* by Stephen R. Covey for getting inside another person's frame of reference through empathic listening.

There are no roadmaps to follow. No instructions. No how-tos. And no formulas for success. Instead you'll find a collection of contemporary quotes, thought-provoking questions, provocative messages, and practical wisdom in an easy-to-read format.

As you turn these pages, take the words of advice to heart, mind, body, and soul. Think about what you read. Ponder how and what it would take to communicate more effectively in your everyday life. Let the wisdom inspire you to become a better listener by using empathy to transform and enrich your relationships.

In essence, make it a habit to seek first to understand, then to be understood.

HABIT 5: SEEK FIRST TO UNDERSTAND, THEN TO BE UNDERSTOOD®

Listen to people sincerely.

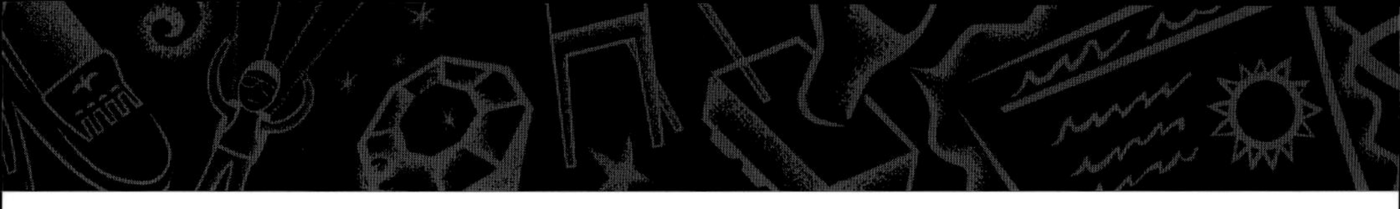

COMMUNICATION

Before problems come up, before you try to evaluate and prescribe, before you try to present your own ideas—seek to understand. When we really, deeply understand each other, we open the door to creative solutions and third alternatives. Our differences are no longer stumbling blocks to communication and progress.

—STEPHEN R. COVEY, *The 7 Habits of Highly Effective People*

Although the tongue weighs very little,

FEW PEOPLE ARE ABLE TO HOLD IT.

—UNKNOWN

GOOD COMMUNICATION

is stimulating as black coffee, and just as hard to sleep after.

—ANNE MORROW LINDBERGH

It was hard to communicate with you. You were always communicating with yourself. **The line was busy.**

—*MARY, MARY*

Hello, you've reached a person who never listens. Your call is very important to me, but I am too caught up in emotional phone tag to pay attention to you right now. An operator will be with you shortly. While you are waiting, please have the following skills ready: the willingness to deal with my lack of communication skills, my lifelong emotional unavailability, my physical inattention, and my lack of empathy to any of your so-called problems. The ability to always listen to me even if I don't listen to you also helps. And above all, no whining. Before proceeding, please review the following options: **Press 1** to eliminate rejection issues. **Press 2** to relinquish integrity. **Press 3** to destroy all thoughts about sharing. **Press 4** to hang up and automatically have a relationship with someone you can "talk to." If you want to justify your existence, feel your feelings, or play verbal volleyball, please hold. If you want to ask how this makes me feel, please hang up and go directly to the sensitive New-Age therapist of your choice. At any point, you have the option to **press 0** to get a life. I understand that this process can be confusing and I would like to be of assistance, but I'm on the other line disassociating and my radar is turned off. Your call is very important to me. And I will return it but not in this lifetime. Please continue to hold. Or not.

Two may talk together

under the same roof

for many years, yet

never really meet.

—MARY CATHERWOOD

You talkin' to me?

—*TAXI DRIVER*

I feel that if a person has problems communicating, the very least they could do is

SHUT UP.

—TOM LEHRER

MIRROR, MIRROR

Try these conversation starters with your partner or a friend. Have the person repeat back to you what was said. When what was said is understood by both people, say "thank you for understanding" and go on to the next sentence. If what was said is a particularly problematic area of your relationship, stick with one idea at a time and explore it further using this mirror technique.

Lately I've noticed ____________________

I am puzzled by ____________________

I would appreciate it if ____________________

When you (behavior), I feel ____________________

What I want is ____________________

How can we ____________________

What can I do to ____________________

I appreciate your ____________________

What scares me is ____________________

I am at peace when ____________________

If we try to listen, we find it extraordinarily difficult because we are always projecting our opinions and ideas, our prejudices, our backgrounds, our inclinations, our impulses, when they dominate we hardly listen to what is being said...One listens and therefore learns, only in a state of silence.

—KRISHNAMURTI

Why is it

that when anything goes without saying,
it never does?

—MARCELENE COX

The best way to get the last word is to apologize.

EMPATHY

Empathic Listening is so powerful because it gives you accurate data to work with. Instead of projecting your own autobiography and assuming thoughts, feelings, motives, and interpretation, you're dealing with the reality inside another person's head and heart.

—STEPHEN R. COVEY, *The 7 Habits of Highly Effective People*

I think that it's important to know how the water's gone over the dam before you start to describe it.
It helps to have been over the dam yourself.
—E. ANNIE PROULX

Why do people with closed minds always open their mouths?

E M P A T H Y

is walking with another person into the deeper chambers of his self—while still maintaining some separateness. It involves experiencing the feelings of another without losing one's own identity...When a person loses the ability to separate his own feelings from the feelings of the other person, he is no longer empathic.

—ROBERT BOLTON

Compassion is the ultimate and most meaningful embodiment of emotional maturity. It is through compassion that a person achieves the highest peak and the deepest reach in his or her search for self-fulfillment.

—ARTHUR JERSILD

If I want your opinion,

I'll ask you to fill out the necessary forms.

The people we most enjoy talking to are ones who show empathy for us—who make clear they relate to what we're feeling as well as what we're saying...All the best conversationalists among TV hosts share this quality. I call them **"commiserators."**

—LARRY KING

When you ask a woman what she's feeling and she doesn't respond, it means:

a. She didn't hear you.

b. She fainted.

c. Nothing. It's just a silly stereotype that women want to talk about their feelings all the time.

d. That slamming door you heard twenty minutes ago was her leaving.

[The answer is b. She fainted from surprise.]

—THE NATIONAL STANDARDIZED LOVE TEST

Listening

is the art by which we use empathy
to reach across the space between
us. Passive attention doesn't work.

—MICHAEL P. NICHOLS

SAY WHAT YOU MEAN,

MEAN WHAT YOU SAY,

BUT DON'T SAY IT MEAN.

How to Become an EMPATHIC LISTENER

1. Practice saying, "Take your time, I'm listening," and really mean it.

2. Set aside your own agenda.

3. Be available and receptive emotionally as well as through body language.

4. Try to appreciate the other person's point of view.

5. Listen without being in a hurry to take over.

6. Try to imagine yourself in the other's place; feel what the speaker feels.

7. Help draw out thoughts and feelings by asking questions.

8. Have the speaker elaborate for further understanding.

9. Say, "Let me make sure I understand…" and then restate the issue.

10. Be sensitive to the speaker's feelings.

One reason a dog can be such a comfort when you're feeling blue is that he doesn't try to find out why.

—UNKNOWN

LISTENING

Knowing I need to listen and knowing how to listen is not enough. Unless I want to listen, unless I have the desire, it won't be a habit in my life.

—STEPHEN R. COVEY, *The 7 Habits of Highly Effective People*

When you're listening to someone,

CALM YOUR INNER CHATTER.

Forget about how you're going to respond. And, most important of all, bite your tongue hard when you want to say, "That's not how I would do it."

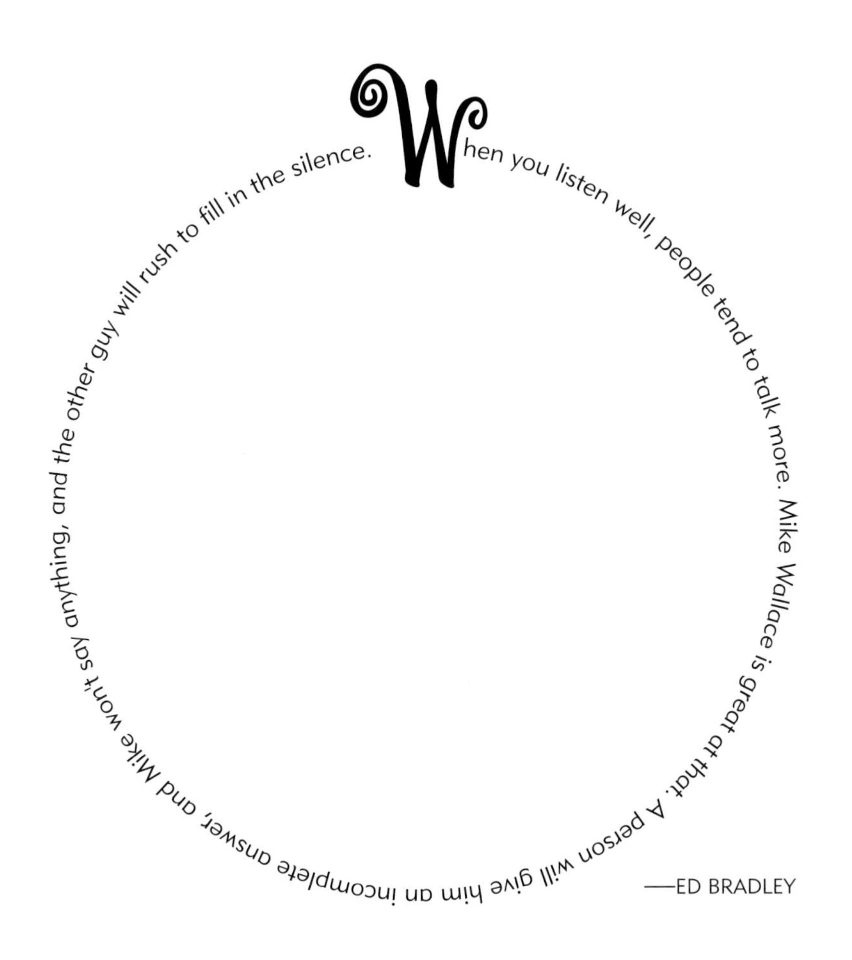

When you listen well, people tend to talk more. Mike Wallace is great at that. A person will give him an incomplete answer, and Mike won't say anything, and the other guy will rush to fill in the silence.

—ED BRADLEY

Genuine listening means suspending memory, desire, and judgment—and, for a few moments at least, existing for the other person.

—MICHAEL P. NICHOLS

YOU HAVE THE RIGHT TO REMAIN SILENT,

so please feel free to do so while I'm talking.

The opposite
of talking
isn’t listening.
The opposite
of talking
is waiting.

—FRAN LEIBOWITZ

We learn but only when we are silent from within do we really speak clearly.

—SEAL

BE FULLY PRESENT.

Empathic Listening takes time. But it doesn't take anywhere near as much time as it takes to back up and correct misunderstandings when you're already miles down the road, to redo, to live with unexpressed and unsolved problems, to deal with the results of not **giving people psychological air.**

—STEPHEN R. COVEY

Guidelines for Influential Listening

1. Listen with a head-heart connection—pause.

2. Listen with the intent of understanding.

3. Listen for the message and the message behind the message.

4. Listen for both content and feelings.

5. Listen with your eyes—your hearing will be improved.

6. Listen for others' interests, not just their position.

7. Listen for what they are saying and not saying.

8. Listen with empathy and acceptance.

9. Listen for the areas where they are afraid and hurt.

10. Listen as you would like to be listened to.

—ERIC ALLENBAUGH

Isn't it boring...how people always want to tell you their own stories instead of listening to yours? I suppose that's why psychiatrists are better than friends; the paid listener doesn't interrupt with his own experiences.

—HELEN VAN SYKE

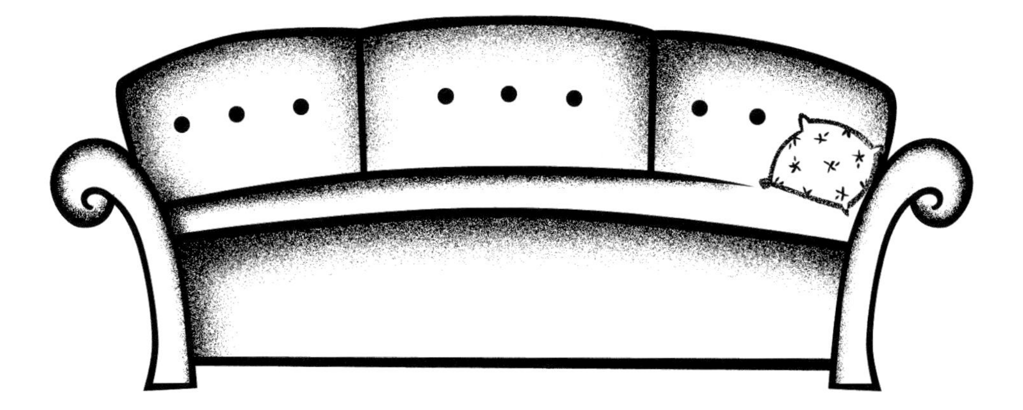

A sympathetic ear is a terrible thing to waste.

PERCEPTION

As you learn to listen deeply to other people, you will discover tremendous differences in perception. You will also begin to appreciate the impact that these differences can have as people try to work together in interdependent situations.

—STEPHEN R. COVEY, *The 7 Habits of Highly Effective People*

I REALLY DON'T WANT TO

COMMUNICATE.

I JUST WANT TO BE

UNDERSTOOD.

—©ASHLEIGH BRILLIANT

A lot of seemingly inexplicable behavior—signs of coming closer or pulling back—occurs because others react to our style of talking in ways that lead them to conclusions we never suspect. **Many of our motives, so obvious to us, are never perceived by the people we talk to.** Many instances of rudeness, stubbornness, inconsiderateness, or refusal to cooperate are really caused by differences in conversational style.

—DEBORAH TANNEN

The biggest
jump in the world
is jumping
to conclusion.

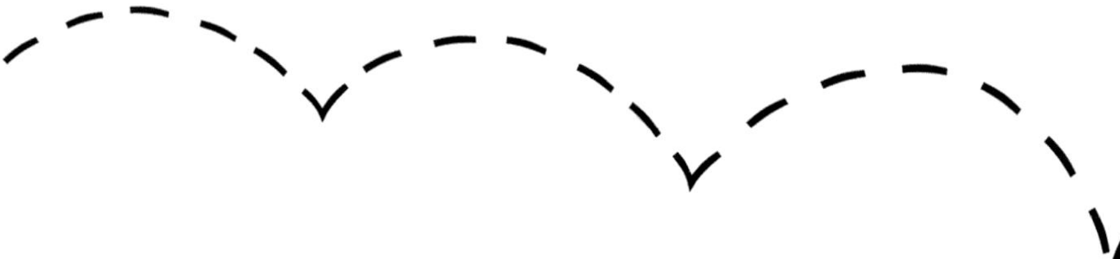

When someone close brings up a recurring issue, some people get upset and say something like, **"How many times do we have to go through this?"** Such retorts make sense if you feel that the speaker's complaints mean that you're responsible or that it's your job to solve whatever problem the person is complaining about. But is it really your job?...Once you understand that other people's talking about what's bothering them makes them feel better simply for being listened to, you can relax, knowing that just listening without becoming reactive can make both of you feel better.

—MICHAEL P. NICHOLS

Ever stop to think,
and forget to start again?

I often ponder over the nature of true human sincerity,

true transparency.

It is a rare and difficult thing; and how much it depends on the person who is listening to us! There are those who pull down the barriers and make the way smooth; there are those who force the doors and enter our territory like invaders; there are those who barricade us in, shut us in upon ourselves, dig ditches and throw up walls around us; there are those who set us out of tune and listen only to our false notes; there are those for whom we always remain strangers, speaking an unknown tongue. And when it is our turn to listen, which of these are we?

—UNKNOWN

Without good communication, a relationship is merely a hollow vessel carrying you along on a frustrating journey fraught with the perils of confusion, projection, and misunderstanding.

—CHÉRIE CARTER-SCOTT

Let go

of your attachment to being right,
and suddenly your mind is more
open. You're able to benefit from the
unique viewpoints of others, without
being crippled by your own judgment.

—RALPH MARSTON

When you measure someone's worth, put the tape around the heart instead of the head.

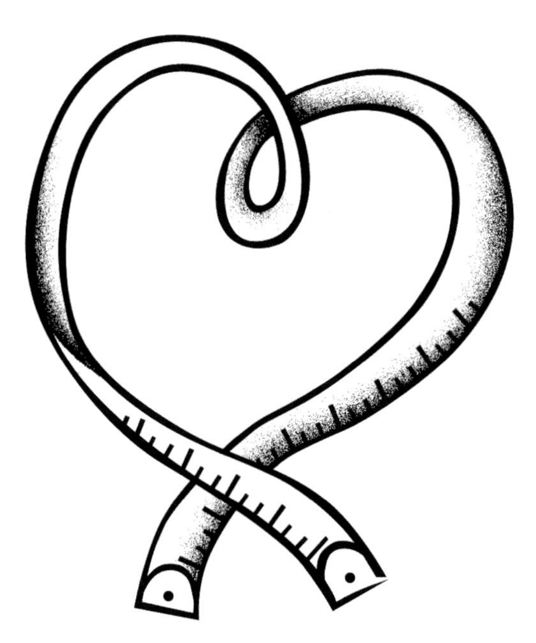

Ya know?

During a typical 15-minute radio program, the words "ya know" are uttered a whopping 61 times. Listen for it in your conversations. You're probably not even aware you're saying the innocuous phrase more than a hundred times a day. Once attuned to how unprofessional it makes you sound, it will be easier to curb your desire to, ya know, say it.

Can you hear what is NOT being said?

TRUST

Trust is the highest form of human motivation. It brings out the very best in people. But it takes time and patience, and it doesn't preclude the necessity to train and develop people so that their competency can rise to the level of that trust.

—STEPHEN R. COVEY, *The 7 Habits of Highly Effective People*

You have to choose

the voice you are

going to trust.

You can't listen to everyone.

—ALICE HOFFMAN

It was enough
just to sit there
without words.

—LOUISE ERDRICH

The flip side

to being attracted to unavailable people is how bored you are by available people. Available people are terrifying because they want to hang around long enough to know you, to like you, to accept you. The problem is not that you attract unavailable people—the problem is that you give them your number.

—MARIANNE WILLIAMSON

TOP TEN LIES OF ALL TIME

10

I'll call you.

9

I'm working late tonight.

8

I'm (insert age—usually five years younger)

7

I weigh (insert weight—usually ten pounds less).

6

Sure, I'll take care of it.

5

It's not you. It's me.

4

I promise I won't tell anyone.

3

I got caught in traffic.

2

Let's do lunch sometime.

1

TRUST ME.

Is it safe for me to be me when I am with you?

When you break your word, you break the one thing that cannot be mended.

—UNKNOWN

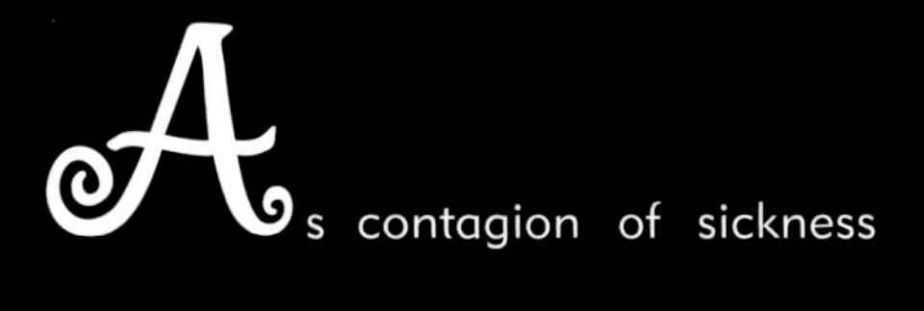

As contagion of sickness makes sickness, contagion of trust can make trust.

—MARIANNE MOORE

Increasing credibility requires

OPENNESS.

Hidden agendas will destroy trust.

—JUDITH M. BARDWICK

Are You a Dirt Devil or an Antigossip Angel?

You don't need to become a black hole of information to get friends and coworkers to trust you with their secrets. In fact, there are times in your life when mum is not the word. If you hold back information that could help someone, they won't be in your life for long. You've got to know when to be up-front and when to zip your lip. On the other hand, if you're a chronic dirt disher and cannot keep a secret to save your life, imagine the person you're talking about standing behind you overhearing every word. Now, a little dirt dishing is normal as long as you're not using a backhoe. In fact, that just may bury your most important relationships.

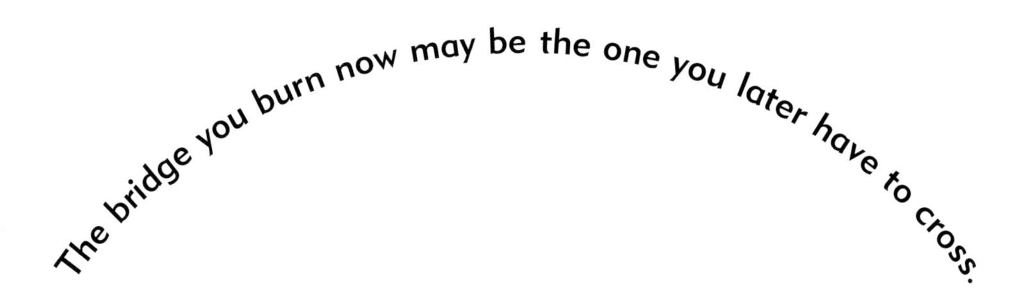
The bridge you burn now may be the one you later have to cross.

You're not going to make me have a bad day. If there's oxygen on earth and I'm breathing, it's going to be a good day.

—COTTON FITZSIMMONS

CLARITY

When you present your own ideas clearly, specifically, visually, and most important, contextually—in the context of a deep understanding of others' paradigms and concerns—you significantly increase the credibility of your ideas.

—STEPHEN R. COVEY, *The 7 Habits of Highly Effective People*

I personally think we developed language because of

our deep inner need to complain.

—JANE WAGNER

Why can't we just say what we mean?

If something we said can be interpreted two ways,

and one of the ways makes you sad and angry,

we meant the other one.

—*RULES THAT MEN WISH EVERY WOMAN KNEW*

You tell your husband a long list of home improvement projects you would like to see done, and he says, "Yes, dear." In this context, "yes dear" means

a. Yes, dear.

b. Perhaps, dear.

c. Yeah, right.

d. Next time marry a contractor.

[The answer is **d**, unless you are already married to a contractor, in which case the answer is **c**.]

—*THE NATIONAL STANDARDIZED LOVE TEST*

person

who talks fast

often says things

she hasn't thought of yet.

—CARON WARNER LIEBER

AMBIVALENT?

Well, yes and no.

In communicating, your purpose is
not to judge but to understand.

In order to get what we want, we must say what we mean. In order to say what we mean, we must know what we want. When we know what we want, we can think and speak positively with

great expectations.

—IYANLA VANZANT

Don't just tell someone you want and need "more" from him or her and then let it go. It's not specific enough. You must be clear about what "more" is before anyone else can be clear about it.

VALIDATION

Next to physical survival, the greatest need of a human being is psychological survival—to be understood, to be affirmed, to be validated, to be appreciated.

—STEPHEN R. COVEY, *The 7 Habits of Highly Effective People*

It is a rare person who wants to hear what he doesn't want to hear.

—DICK CAVETT

My lover and I will be out for a ride.

He'll be driving and say,
"I'm taking Route 295 to the bridge.
What do you think?"

And I say, **"BERFLEGUMP HIPPLE DIP."**

He'll say,
"I'm hungry. I'm stopping at the diner.
What do you think?"

And I answer, **"QUIDDY DIDDLE QUANK BLURP."**

Why am I talking gibberish?

Because I want to be understood. He's one of those new sensitive kind of guys, who knows enough to ask me what I think—but he hasn't quite evolved to the point where he cares about the answer.

—FLASH ROSENBERG

I love that you get cold when it's 71 degrees out. I love that it takes you an hour and a half to order a sandwich. I love that you get a little crinkle above your nose when you're looking at me like I'm nuts. I love that after a day with you I can still smell your perfume on my clothes. And I love that you are the last person I want to talk to before I go to sleep at night. And that's not because I'm lonely and it's not because it's New Year's Eve. I came here tonight because when you realize you want to spend the rest of your life with somebody, you want the rest of your life to start as soon as possible.

—*WHEN HARRY MET SALLY*

Never let a problem

to be solved become

more important than

a person to be loved.

—BARBARA JOHNSON

When you offer your opinion or give advice and the listener doesn't follow it, did the person really ask you for your guidance?

Or did you just assume

he or she would appreciate your all-knowing-all-the-time advice?

A piece of us is in every person we can ever meet.

—STEPHEN R. COVEY

If anything goes bad, I did it.

If anything goes semi-good, we did it.

If anything goes real good, then you did it.

That's all it takes to get people to win football games for you.

—PAUL "BEAR" BRYANT

The winners in life think

constantly in terms of

I CAN,

I WILL,

and

I AM.

Losers, on the other hand,

concentrate their waking thoughts

on what they should have or would

have done or what they can't do.

—DENIS WAITLEY

Veni, Vidi, Verily — I Came, I Saw, I Concurred.

ACKNOWLEDGMENT

The more deeply you understand other people, the more you will appreciate them, the more reverent you will feel about them. To touch the soul of another human being is to walk on holy ground.

—STEPHEN R. COVEY, *The 7 Habits of Highly Effective People*

I've discovered more ways I'm right and you're wrong

—aren't you anxious to hear them?

—©ASHLEIGH BRILLIANT

Don't look over

other people's shoulders.

Look into their eyes.

Don't talk at your children.

Take their faces in your hands and talk to them.

Don't make love to a body, make love to a person.

—LEO BUSCAGLIA

PUTTING UP WITH PUT-DOWNS

The next time you're hit by an unsolicited opinion or insult, thank him or her for the opinion and move on. It's no fun for put-down artists if they don't get a mortified response from you. The last thing you want to do is trade barbs. Remind yourself how sad it is when someone resorts to cruelty to feel better. Plus, a thank you puts you in the power position and the insult loses its impact.

Can we talk?

I'm rarely at a loss for words. As far as I'm concerned, talking is a natural biological function, like breathing—I do it all the time. Yet my husband can hold his breath for hours even days at a time. The silence is deafening. "Is something bothering you?" I ask, even though I realize that trying to pull words from the mouth of a man in the midst of a mute spell is as pointless as trying to make a telephone call when the line is dead.

—MARGO KAUFMAN

I just want revenge.

Is that so bad?

In a word,

YES.

What does "meet me halfway" really mean? When we get halfway, what are we going to do? What lies ahead of us? Who is going to take the first step beyond the halfway point? When someone tells you, "I'm here for you" or "I'll be there for you," what are they talking about?

What are you doing there when I'm over here?...Until we make a commitment to communicate clearly and effectively in our relationships, we will be halfway there with nothing happening here.

—IYANLA VANZANT

There's no limit to what we can accomplish
—if we don't mind who gets the credit.

TELEVISION has proved that people will look at anything rather than each other.

—ANN LANDERS

Most of us know how to say nothing but few of us know when.

INTERPRETATION

All the well-meaning advice in the world won't amount to a hill of beans if we're not addressing the real problem. And we'll never get to the problem if we're so caught up in our own autobiography that we don't see the world from another point of view.

—STEPHEN R. COVEY, *The 7 Habits of Highly Effective People*

The one prediction that **never** comes true is,

"You'll thank me for telling you this."

—JUDITH MARTIN

What you see and hear depends a good deal on where you are standing; it also depends on what kind of a person you are.

—C. S. LEWIS

Use

"BUT"

and

"SHOULD"

sparingly.

You ask a woman to dinner and she says, "Sorry, I have to stay home and exfoliate." In this context, exfoliate means:

a. Rub a slightly abrasive cream across my facial pores so as to slough off the dead skin cells

b. Get ready for a date with someone else.

c. Watch *Ally McBeal*, eat fudge, and ask the Fates why no one really cool ever asks you out.

[Either **b** or **c** may be correct. If you said **a**, what are you, a guy or an Avon lady?]

—*THE NATIONAL STANDARDIZED LOVE TEST*

If you want to be happy,

BE.

—LEO TOLSTOY

The true human

is someone who is

aware, someone

who is, moment by

moment, totally and

completely merged

with life. Out of that

capacity of inner and

outer listening comes

the quality of humility.

—JOSEPH RAEL

What does "It would take too long to explain" really mean?

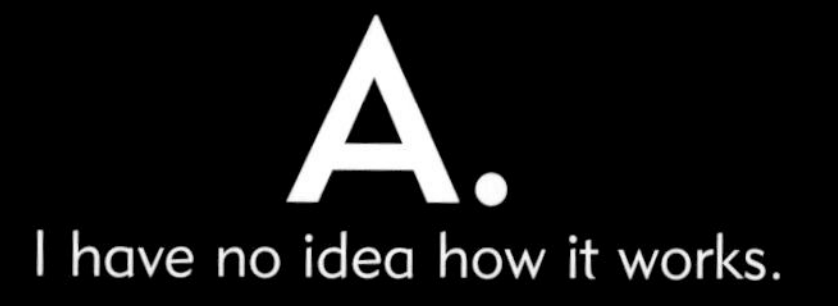

I have no idea how it works.

If we are to have the courage to be ourselves, to stand squarely on our own two feet, then we must accept and acknowledge that other people are themselves and entitled to their own unique points of view. The idea is not to distance ourselves from others but to let them be themselves while we continue to be ourselves... Trying harder to understand the other person's perspective takes effort, but it isn't just a skill to be studied and practiced. Hearing someone out is an expression of

caring enough to listen.

—MICHAEL P. NICHOLS

It is better to ask some of the questions than to know all the answers.

—JAMES THURBER

I worry I will wake up one morning to find that I am half of one of those couples I keep seeing in commercials who have heartfelt, earnest talks about breakfast cereal, and who actually share special moments discussing raisins.

—MERRILL MARKOE

If it's always your way or the highway, maybe it's time for a lane change.

PRESENTATION

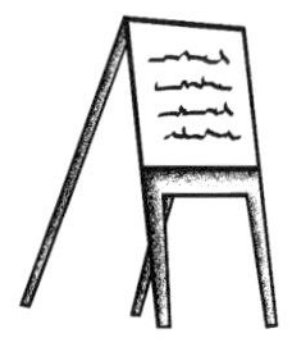

The more authentic you become, particularly regarding personal experiences and even self doubts, the more people can relate to you and feel safe to express themselves...producing new insights, learnings, excitement, and a sense of adventure that keeps the process going.

—STEPHEN R. COVEY, *The 7 Habits of Highly Effective People*

In ten years on the right coast after a lifetime on the left, I fear I've become a hybrid, unfit for either. I move too fast for California, but I'm too cheerful for New York. (Although a couple more years here should take care of that.) Californians think I'm rude because I've picked up a New York practice that I call "participatory listening" and they call "interrupting." New Yorkers assume I suffered some sort of early childhood citrus-induced neural damage that causes me to wait until they're nearly finished with a sentence before I respond.

—JUDITH STONE

How you express criticism is important. Let the other person know that you want to talk at an appointed time rather than starting a fight. Be sensitive and calm. Talk about your feelings not the other person's shortcomings. Remind yourself what you have in common, instead of what separates you.

THE EARLY BIRD MAY GET THE WORM,
BUT THE SECOND MOUSE GETS THE CHEESE.

You simply cannot communicate enough. Experts say that you have to tell the average adult something six times before it is internalized. The challenge becomes communicating a message in such a creative way that it only has to be told once.

—BARBARA A. GANZ

I have come to believe over and over again that what is most important to me must be spoken, made verbal and shared, even at the risk of having it bruised or misunderstood.

That the speaking profits me,

beyond any other effect.

—AUDRE LORDE

DIPLOMACY

is not the art of letting
someone have your way.

WHAT THE Best Talkers HAVE IN COMMON

- They look at things from a new angle, taking unexpected points of view on familiar subjects.
- They have broad horizons. They think about, and talk about, a wide range of issues and experiences beyond their own daily lives.
- They are enthusiastic, displaying a passion for what they're doing with their lives and an interest in what you're saying to them at that moment.
- They don't talk about themselves all the time.
- They are curious. They ask, "Why?" They want to know more about what you're telling them.
- They empathize. They try to put themselves in your place, to relate to what you're saying.
- They have a sense of humor. And they don't mind using it on themselves. In fact, the best conversationalists frequently tell stories on themselves.
- They have their own style of talking.

—LARRY KING

Each person has a literature inside them. But when people lose language, when they have to experiment with putting their thoughts together on the spot—that's what I love most. That's where character lives.

—ANNA DEAVERE SMITH

Other people may complicate our lives, but life without them would be unbearably desolate... **None of us can be truly human in isolation.** The qualities that make us human emerge only in the ways we relate to other people.

—HAROLD KUSHNER

About Franklin Covey

Franklin Covey is the world's leading time management and life leadership company. Based on proven principles, our services and products are used by more than 15 million people worldwide. We work with a wide variety of clients, Fortune 500 material, as well as smaller companies, communities, and organizations. You may know us from our world-renowned Franklin Planner or any of our books in the 7 Habits series. By the way, Franklin Covey books have sold over 15 million copies worldwide—over 1½ million each year. But what you may not know about Franklin Covey is we also offer leadership training, motivational workshops, personal coaching, audiotapes and videotapes, and *PRIORITIES* magazine just to name a few.

Let Us Know What You Think

We'd love to hear your suggestions or comments about *Trust: Sharing Ideas, Insights, and Understanding* or any of our Portable 7 Habits books. All seven books in the series will be published in 2000.

www.franklincovey.com/portable7

The Portable 7 Habits
Franklin Covey
MS0733-CK
2200 West Parkway Boulevard
Salt Lake City, Utah 84119-2331 USA

1-800-952-6839
International (801) 229-1333 Fax (801) 229-1233

PERMISSIONS

Reprinted with permission of Ashleigh Brilliant.
Copyright ©2000 Ashleigh Brilliant.
www.ashleighbrillant.com

Reprinted with permission of Flash Rosenberg. Excerpt from the book "Creme de la Femme" by Anne Safran Dalin, published by Random House. Originally the piece was a cartoon, and it is part of the author's one-woman comic slide performance, "Camping in the Bewilderness".

Excerpt from *Wake-Up Calls: You Don't Have to Sleepwalk Through Your Life, Love, or Career!* by Eric Allenbaugh. Published 1994 Simon and Schuster. Reprinted with permission. All rights reserved.

Reprinted from *How to Talk to Anyone, Anytime, Anywhere: The Secrets of Good Communication* by Larry King with Bill Gilbert. Copyright ©1994 Crown Publishers. Reprinted with permission of Crown Publishers.

The National Standardized Love Test by Annie Pigeon. Copyright ©2000 by Annie Pigeon. Used by permission of Adams Media Corporation. All rights reserved.

RECOMMENDED READING

Barbach, Lonnie. *50 Ways to Please Your Lover while You Please Yourself*. Dutton, 1997.

Bolton, Robert. *People Skills: How to Assert Yourself, Listen to Others, and Resolve Conflicts*. Touchstone, 1979.

Breathnach, Sarah Ban. *Simple Abundance: A Daybook of Comfort and Joy*. Warner Books, 1995.

Carter-Scott, Chérie. *If Love Is a Game, These Are the Rules*. Broadway Books, 1999.

Covey, Stephen R. *The 7 Habits of Highly Effective People*. Simon & Schuster, 1989.

——. *Living the 7 Habits*. Simon & Schuster, 1999.

Dimitrius, Jo-Ellan, and Mark Mazzarella. *Reading People: How to Understand People and Predict Their Behavior—Anytime, Anyplace*. Random House, 1999.

Evans, Patricia. *The Verbally Abusive Relationship: How to Recognize It and How to Respond*. Adams Media Corporation, 1996.

Faber, Adele, and Elaine Mazlish. *How to Talk So Kids Will Listen and Listen So Kids Will Talk*. Avon Books, 1999.

Gray, John. *Men Are from Mars, Women Are from Venus: A Practical Guide for Improving Communication and Getting What You Want in Your Relationships*. HarperTrade, 1992.

King, Larry, with Bill Gilbert. *How to Talk to Anyone, Anytime, Anywhere*. Crown Trade Paperbacks, 1994.

Leiberman, David J. *Never Be Lied to Again: How to Get the Truth in 5 Minutes or Less in Any Conversation or Situation*. St. Martin's Press, 1998.

McGraw, Phillip C. *Relationship Rescue: A Seven-Step Strategy for Reconnecting with Your Partner*. Hyperion, 2000.

McKenna, Colleen. *Powerful Communication Skills: How to Communicate with Confidence*. Career Press, 1998.

Nichols, Michael P. *The Lost Art of Listening: How Learning to Listen Can Improve Relationships*. Guilford Press, 1996.

Rosen, Mark. *Thank You for Being Such a Pain: Spiritual Guidance for Dealing With Difficult People*. Harmony Books, 1998.

Stettner, Morey. *The Art of Winning Conversation*. Prentice Hall, 1995.

——. *The Art of Winning Conversation: Proven Techniques for Personal and Professional Success*. Fine Communications, 1999.

Stone, Douglas, Bruce Patton, and Sheila Heen. *Difficult Conversations: How to Discuss What Matters Most*. Penguin USA, 1999.

Tannen, Deborah. *You Just Don't Understand: Women and Men in Conversation*. Ballantine Books, 1990.

——. *That's Not What I Meant: How Conversational Style Makes or Breaks Relationships*. Ballentine Books, 1986.

VanZant, Iyanla. *Faith in the Valley*. Simon & Schuster, 1998.